EXPLORING SPACE

# The Moon

by Colleen Sexton

Consultant:
Duane Quam, M.S. Physics
Chair, Minnesota State
Academic Science Standards
Writing Committee

BELLWETHER MEDIA · MINNEAPOLIS, MN

Note to Librarians, Teachers, and Parents:

**Blastoff! Readers** are carefully developed by literacy experts and combine standards-based content with developmentally appropriate text.

**Level 1** provides the most support through repetition of high-frequency words, light text, predictable sentence patterns, and strong visual support.

**Level 2** offers early readers a bit more challenge through varied simple sentences, increased text load, and less repetition of high-frequency words.

**Level 3** advances early-fluent readers toward fluency through increased text and concept load, less reliance on visuals, longer sentences, and more literary language.

**Level 4** builds reading stamina by providing more text per page, increased use of punctuation, greater variation in sentence patterns, and increasingly challenging vocabulary.

**Level 5** encourages children to move from "learning to read" to "reading to learn" by providing even more text, varied writing styles, and less familiar topics.

Whichever book is right for your reader, Blastoff! Readers are the perfect books to build confidence and encourage a love of reading that will last a lifetime!

This edition first published in 2010 by Bellwether Media, Inc.

No part of this publication may be reproduced in whole or in part without written permission of the publisher. For information regarding permissions, write to Bellwether Media, Inc., Attention: Permissions Department, 5357 Penn Avenue South, Minneapolis, MN 55419.

Library of Congress Cataloging-in-Publication Data

Sexton, Colleen A., 1967-
The moon / by Colleen Sexton.
p. cm. – (Blastoff! readers. Exploring space)
Includes bibliographical references and index.
Summary: "Introductory text and full-color images explore the physical characteristics of the moon in space. Intended for students in kindergarten through third grade"–Provided by publisher.
ISBN 978-1-60014-401-1 (hardcover : alk. paper)
1. Moon–Juvenile literature. I. Title.
QB582.S47 2010
523.3–dc22
2009037988

Text copyright © 2010 by Bellwether Media, Inc.
Printed in the United States of America, North Mankato, MN.

010110       1149

# Contents

The moon is the largest and brightest object in the night sky.

It is closer to Earth than the sun or any planet. The moon is about 239,000 miles (385,000 kilometers) away.

It takes the moon 29.5 days to **orbit** Earth. The same side of the moon always faces Earth.

Moonlight is light from the sun. Sunlight bounces off the moon and shines on Earth.

The part of the moon that shines changes as the moon orbits Earth.

On Earth it looks like the moon is a different shape each night. These shapes are called **phases**.

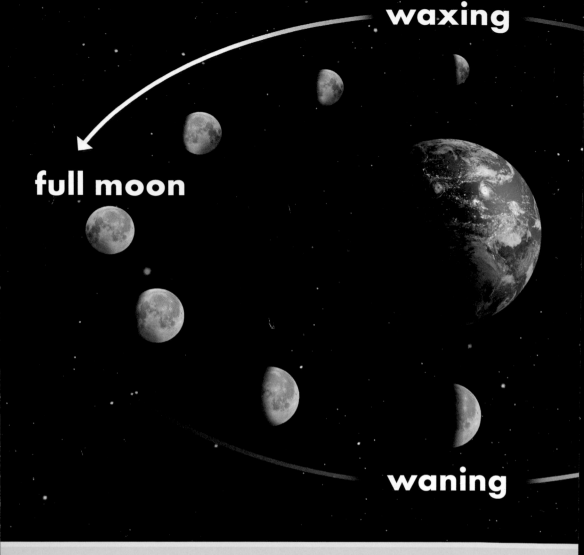

waxing

full moon

waning

First a small curve of the moon appears. It **waxes** each night until it is a **full moon**.

**new moon**

Then the moon **wanes** each night.
It is called a **new moon** when it
seems to disappear.

There are light
and dark areas
on the moon.
The dark areas
are smooth plains
called **maria**.

The light areas are **highlands**. Tall mountains rise from the highlands. Some rocks there are bigger than a house!

13

The moon has thousands of
bowl-shaped holes called **craters**.
Most of the craters formed when
**meteorites** crashed into the moon.

Some craters are smaller than a basketball. The largest are more than 1,000 miles (1,610 kilometers) wide.

Gray dust covers almost
everything on the moon.
In some places the dust is
65 feet (20 meters) deep!

The moon does not have an **atmosphere**. There is no air or weather on the moon. The sky is black all the time.

The moon is a quiet place. Sound travels through air. Without air there is no sound on the moon.

The moon gets very hot and very cold. The temperature rises to 265° Fahrenheit (130° Celsius) in sunlight. It drops to -310°F (-190°C) when the sun sets.

In 1969, people visited the moon for the first time. **Astronauts** collected moon rocks to study back on Earth.

The astronauts left footprints on the moon. The footprints are still there today!

# Glossary

**astronauts**—people who have been trained to fly aboard a space shuttle and work in space

**atmosphere**—the gases around an object in space; the moon does not have an atmosphere.

**craters**—holes made when meteorites or other space objects crash into moons, planets, or other objects

**full moon**—the phase in which the moon appears to be a glowing circle

**highlands**—areas with hills and mountains that are the lightest areas of the moon

**maria**—smooth, flat plains that are the darkest areas of the moon; maria are craters that filled with lava that later hardened.

**meteorites**—pieces of rock or other matter that have fallen from space

**new moon**—the phase in which the moon cannot be seen

**orbit**—to travel around the sun or object in space; the moon completes an orbit of Earth every 29.5 days; that amount of time is called a lunar month.

**phases**—the different shapes the moon seems to have as it orbits Earth

**wanes**—shrinks in size; the amount of sunlight shining off of the moon decreases as the moon wanes.

**waxes**—grows in size; the amount of sunlight shining off of the moon increases as the moon waxes.

# To Learn More

## AT THE LIBRARY

Carle, Eric. *Papa, Please Get the Moon for Me*. New York, N.Y.: Simon & Shuster, 1986.

Haddon, Mark. *Footprints on the Moon*. Somerville, Mass.: Candlewick Press, 2009.

McNulty, Faith. *If You Decide to Go to the Moon*. New York, N.Y.: Scholastic, 2005.

## ON THE WEB

Learning more about the moon is as easy as 1, 2, 3.

1. Go to www.factsurfer.com.

2. Enter "the moon" into the search box.

3. Click the "Surf" button and you will see a list of related Web sites.

With factsurfer.com, finding more information is just a click away.

## BLASTOFF! JIMMY CHALLENGE

Blastoff! Jimmy is hidden somewhere in this book. Can you find him? If you need help, you can find a hint at the bottom of page 24.

# Index

The images in this book are reproduced through the courtesy of: Juan Martinez, front cover, pp: 4, 6 (small), 6-7, 10-11; NASA, pp. 5, 20, FIT, pp. 8-9; Christophe Luhenoff, p. 12 (small); Stocktrek Images, pp. 12-13; Mark Garlick / Science Photo Library, p. 14; Photolibrary, p. 15; Jason Reed, pp. 16-17; Jason Ware / Science Photo Library, p. 18; Julian Baum / Science Photo Library, p. 19; Detlev van Ravenswaay, p. 21.

**Blastoff! Jimmy Challenge (from page 23).**
Hint: Go to page 13 and "rock" on.